THE SPOOKIEST HALLOWEEN EVER!

BY TEDDY SLATER

ILLUSTRATED BY ETHAN LONG

SCHOLASTIC INC.

NEW YORK TORONTO LONDON AUCKLAND SYDNEY
MEXICO CITY NEW DELHI HONG KONG BUENOS AIRES

For the newlyweds, Brian and Lila M.
—T.S.

For all of the wonderful children
who have tricked or treated us over the years.
"Boo!" to you all!
—E.L.

ISBN 0-439-87982-5

12 11 10 9 8 7 8 9 10 11/0

BOOK DESIGN BY JANET KUSMIERSKI

Printed in the U.S.A.
First printing, October 2006

A pale moon is rising on Halloween night.
The ghosts have all gathered to give you a fright.

Ghosts are here, ghosts are there.
On All Hallow's Eve, you'll see ghosts everywhere.

Down the street, trick-or-treating,
doorbell-ringing, candy-eating...

In the shadowy night, they come to your door.

You can give them some sweets,
but they'll still ask for more.

They float down the street
to a house made of stone.
You can hear the wind wail.
You can hear the ghosts moan.

Lightning flashes. Thunder crashes.
It isn't too late. You can still run back home.

A Halloween party's about to begin.
Come in, if you dare.
You'll find more ghosts within.

Help yourselves, please.
There are goodies to eat,

toad-jelly pudding—
a most tasty treat.

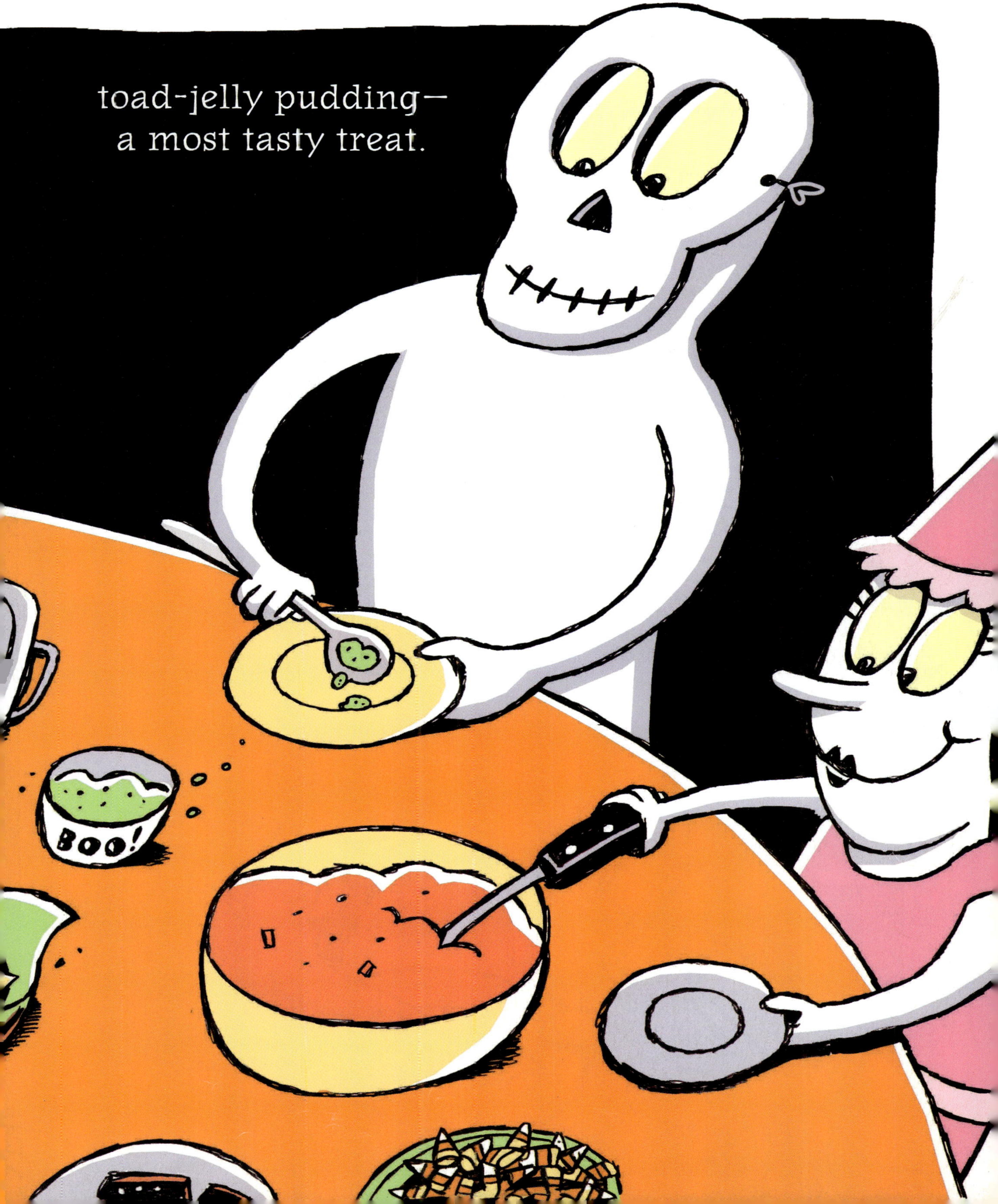

Poached lizards' gizzards,
a fine monster stew—
they're all quite nutritious,
and so yummy, too!

It's time for some games now.
Let's go, everyone.
Pin-the-Wart-on-the-Witch
is oh, so much fun.

Green apples bob in a big wooden tub.

Lean down and grab one.

Glub!

Glub!

Glub!

Glub!

Jack-o'-lanterns glowing bright.
Candles gleaming in the night.
Black cat creeping up the stairs.
Someone knocks, but no one's there!

Skeletons dance to a cool boogie beat.
Rattling their bones and stomping their feet.

Witches, wizards, goblins, ghouls,
pirates, fairies, mummies,
werewoooooolves.

Nobody here is quite what they seem.
And that's the whole point...

Have a happy Halloween!
BOO!